Also by the same author, and available in Coronet Books:

You're a Brave Man, Charlie Brown

Selected Cartoons from
You Can Do It, Charlie Brown, Vol. II

Charles M. Schulz

CORONET BOOKS
Hodder Fawcett, London

Coronet edition 1970
Ninth impression 1977

Printed in Great Britain for
Hodder Fawcett Ltd., Mill Road, Dunton Green,
Sevenoaks, Kent (Editorial Office:
47 Bedford Square, London, WC1 3DP) by
C. Nicholls & Company Ltd,
The Philips Park Press, Manchester

ISBN 0 340 12838 0

DEAR SANTA CLAUS, I KNOW YOU ARE A BUSY MAN.

MAKE IT EASY ON YOURSELF. THIS YEAR JUST BRING ME MONEY.

I DON'T WANT YOU TO WASTE YOUR TIME THINKING ABOUT WHAT TOYS I MIGHT LIKE.

PREFERABLY TENS AND TWENTIES.

WHAT AM I GOING TO DO, CHARLIE BROWN?

MY "BLANKET-HATING" GRANDMA IS COMING TO VISIT US...SHE'LL BE ON ME THE FIRST THING ABOUT THIS BLANKET...SHE'LL HOUND ME TO DEATH...

SHE SAYS SHE RAISED FIVE CHILDREN OF HER OWN AND THEY DIDN'T HAVE BLANKETS AND NO GRANDCHILD OF HERS IS GOING TO HAVE A BLANKET EITHER!

MAYBE SHE'S CALMED DOWN SINCE THE LAST TIME SHE WAS HERE...

MAYBE THE MOON WILL FALL OUT OF THE SKY!

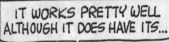

THEIR PARENTS DON'T APPROVE
OF THEIR BEING TOGETHER...

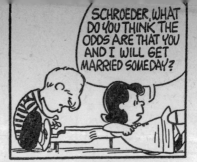

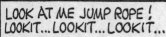

HE THINKS IF HE SITS IN THE RAIN LOOKING PATHETIC, SOME RICH LADY WILL COME ALONG IN A BIG CAR, AND TAKE HIM TO HER HOME TO LIVE A LIFE OF EASE

WHAT SORT OF LIFE DOES HE THINK HE'S LIVING NOW?

FOR ONE THING, I'M SURROUNDED BY SARCASM!

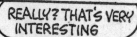

I HATE PLAYING "TEDDY BEAR"!

YOU BOUGHT A NEW KITE, CHARLIE BROWN? THAT'S CRUEL!

YOU'RE GOING TO TAKE THAT SWEET INNOCENT KITE OUT, AND TANGLE IT AROUND SOME TREE? OH, HOW CRUEL!

OR WORSE YET, YOU'RE GOING TO TANGLE IT UP IN SOME TELEPHONE WIRES WHERE IT WILL HANG ALL SUMMER, AND BE BUFFETED BY THE ELEMENTS! HOW CRUEL! OH, HOW INHUMANE!

I'D LIKE TO RETURN A KITE, PLEASE!

I CAN'T LET YOU IN, SNOOPY...
MY MOTHER DOESN'T LIKE THE
SMELL OF A WET DOG...

MY MIND REELS
WITH SARCASTIC
REPLIES!

"SOON HANSEL AND GRETEL CAME TO A LITTLE COTTAGE"

"WHEN THEY GOT QUITE NEAR, THEY SAW THAT THE LITTLE HOUSE WAS MADE OF BREAD AND ROOFED WITH CAKE"

"THE WINDOWS WERE TRANSPARENT SUGAR"

THERE MUST NOT HAVE BEEN A VERY STRICT BUILDING CODE